D0591921

WHY, GOD, WHY?

WHY, GOD, WHY?

*How to Be Delivered
from Confusion*

———

JOYCE
MEYER

WARNER
Faith

NEW YORK   BOSTON   NASHVILLE

Warner Books Edition
Copyright © 1995 by Joyce Meyer
Life In The Word, Inc.
P.O. Box 655
Fenton, Missouri 63026
All rights reserved.

Warner Faith

Time Warner Book Group
1271 Avenue of the Americas, New York, NY 10020
Visit our Web site at www.twbookmark.com.

The Warner Faith name and logo are registered trademarks of Warner Books.

Printed in the United States of America

First Warner Faith Printing: February 2003
10   9   8   7   6   5   4   3   2

ISBN: 0–446–69155–0
LCCN: 2002115637

CONTENTS

❧

Foreword   vii

1   What Causes Confusion?   1

2   Delivered from "Reasonings"   5

3   The Attitude of Faith   9

4   Grace Comes One Day at a Time   13

5   If Only   17

6   What If?   21

7   Don't Be Led by Your Head   25

8   "Reasonings" Cause Deception   31

9   Confusion Steals Your Joy   37

FOREWORD

John 10:10 (AMP) says that the thief comes to steal, kill and destroy, but Jesus came that you might have and *enjoy* life.

Satan would like to rob you of your joy and, therefore, prevent you from enjoying life. But I pray that this book will help you learn how to "let God be God" in your life, so that you can enjoy the abundance of peace and joy that Jesus died for you to have.

1

WHAT CAUSES CONFUSION?

*A*re you confused? Is there something happening in your life right now that you do not understand? Perhaps it is your past, and you just do not understand why your life had to be the way it was. You may be saying, "Why me, God? Why couldn't things have been this way or that way? Why did they have to turn out the way they did? I just don't understand!"

I began to realize that a large number of people suffer tremendously with confusion. I had experienced my share in the past and knew how confusion tormented people, and I began to ponder why people get confused and what they could do to prevent it.

One night I was holding a meeting in Kansas City, and approximately 300 people were in attendance. I felt led to ask how many of them were currently confused over some issue in their life. To my astonishment, I only saw two people who did not raise their hand, and one of them was my husband.

If I saw correctly, that means 298 out of 300 people were confused. That is 99.3 percent. As I began to check with various groups, I found this to be the case almost everywhere. The percentage varied, of course, but was always high.

As I pondered it and asked the Lord to show me what causes confusion, He said, *"Tell them to stop trying to figure everything out, and they will stop being confused."* Now I realize that is exactly why I am not suffering with confusion anymore. I still have plenty of things in my life that I do not understand, but there is a major difference now. God has delivered me from trying to figure everything out. *God has delivered me from reasoning* (the "reasonings" that Second Corinthians 10:5 talks about), so I do not try to figure out the things in my life that I do not understand anymore.

It almost sounds too easy, doesn't it? But there is total freedom from the torment of confusion just by refusing the temptation to figure things out (reasoning). If you really stop and think about it, it does make sense because all this transpires in the region called "the mind."

The mind is the battlefield where our war with Satan is either won or lost. *"God is not the author of confusion"* (1 COR. 14:33)—Satan is. The devil offers us theories and reasonings that are not in line with God's Word. Second Corinthians 10:4, 5 (AMP) says one of the kinds of thinking we will need to eliminate in order to win the war is reasoning. The verses say:

"For the weapons of our warfare are not physical [weapons of flesh and blood], but they are mighty before God for the overthrow and destruction of strongholds,

"[Inasmuch as we] refute arguments and theories and reasonings and every proud and lofty thing that sets itself up against the [true] knowledge of God; and we lead every thought and purpose away captive into the obedience of Christ (the Messiah, the Anointed One)."

2 CORINTHIANS 10:4, 5

If the Word instructs us not to try to figure things out, then we need to obey. And when reasonings come to us, we should bring our thoughts into the obedience of Jesus. These Scriptures say we are in a war, and our warfare, our battle, is largely a mental battle. Satan attacks our minds.

According to these Scriptures, we are dealing with his attacks, with *imaginations*. Did you ever imagine things that were not true or see things on the picture screen of your mind that you knew were improper? *Theories* are various schemes or ideas about how to solve your own problems, and *reasonings* are a probing around with the mind trying to locate answers to questions that only God seems to have.

To sum up this chapter, let us say that confusion is caused by trying to figure out or locate an answer to a situation that only God seems to have. For some reason, it is only known to Him, and He is not telling.

2

❦

DELIVERED FROM "REASONINGS"

*F*irst, you must understand the kind of mind I had before you can truly appreciate my deliverance from reasoning.

Early in life I concluded that to depend on no one, to be independent and to care for oneself, was the safest and best policy. I had it figured out that the least amount of help I had to ask for, the better off I would be because then I would not owe anyone anything. I was tired of being hurt and thought this type of approach would protect me from pain.

I was, of course, wrong; but it took me a long time to realize that and to admit it. Since it took a long time, I spent those years worrying, reasoning, figuring, theorizing, imagining, fretting, being frustrated, upset and on and on the list goes. The more independent we are, the harder it is to trust God or anyone else.

The Lord wants us to be dependent on Him, not independent of Him and dependent on ourselves. The more dependent you are on Christ Jesus, the more you will be able to release things to Him that you do not understand, knowing that He knows, and when the time is right, He will reveal it to you.

Do not confuse this type of an attitude with passivity. We are not to be passive, at least not where faith is concerned. If something happens in your life to you or to a friend and you just do not understand at all what happened or why, you certainly must begin with prayer. Ask the Holy Spirit to give you understanding, to teach you, to shed light and to bring revelation, then wait until He does, knowing that in God's timing He will bring you understanding.[1]

When questions arise in your heart, you may ponder them awhile, but at the precise moment you begin to feel confused, simply thank God that He has the answer, tell Him you are satisfied to know that He knows the answer,

1. Joyce has a book available on God's timing called *When, God, When?*

and tell Him that you trust Him to show you when His time is correct.

You will never be delivered from reasoning and confusion until you adopt—take as your own—this attitude I have been describing. This attitude, by the way, is the *attitude of faith*.

3

❦

THE ATTITUDE OF FAITH

*W*e might refer to faith as a doctrine or an avenue through which we receive from God. In Ephesians 2:8, 9 we see that it is by grace *through faith* that we are saved. Hebrews 11:1 (AMP) says, "Faith is the assurance . . . of the things [we] hope for, being the proof of things [we] do not see." We can describe or define faith in various ways, but I believe a very simple way to look at faith, even examine whether or not we are operating in faith, is to say that "faith has an attitude."

The attitude of faith brings us into rest. Hebrews 4:3 says those who have believed God do enter His rest. Hebrews 4 also says that he who has once entered God's rest (remember, faith is the doorway to rest) has also ceased from the weariness and pain of human labors.

(Verse 10.) *Reasoning is labor* and takes you into confusion, not rest.

The attitude of faith says I will cast my care upon Him for He cares for me. (1 PETER 5:7.) It says, *I do not have to know and understand everything that is going on. I am satisfied to know The One Who does know!* (Author's paraphrase.) Spend your time getting to know Him instead of trying to figure out what He is doing.

The attitude of faith does not worry, fret or have anxiety concerning tomorrow because faith understands that wherever it needs to go, even into the unknowns of tomorrow, that Jesus has already been there. Remember, He is the One Who was, Who is and Who is to come. He was there before the foundation of the world was laid. He assisted in creation. He knew you before you were born. He formed you with His own hand in your mother's womb. Not only was He there at the beginning, but *He* is The Beginning, The Alpha.

What about the finish? Does He get things going and then drop out? *No!* He will finish what He has begun. (HEB. 12:2; PHIL. 1:6.) He will be there at the end. He is the End, the Omega. I like to say it like this, "Not only is He the Alpha and Omega, the Beginning and the End, but He is also everything in between."

Assuming Jesus tarries awhile, I have a lot of tomorrows left, and so do you. I am glad to know and to be comforted in knowing that whatever tomorrow holds for me, He holds tomorrow and me in the palm of His hand. (ISA. 49:16.)

The attitude of faith lives one day at a time.

4

꘎

GRACE COMES
ONE DAY AT A TIME

"*R*easonings" either trap us in the past or try to push us into the future. Remember, the Bible says, "*Now* faith is" (HEB. 11:1). If you try to live in the past, life will be hard. He did not call Himself "the great I Was." If you try to live in the future or try to figure out what will happen tomorrow, life will be hard. He did not call Himself "the great I Will Be." But if you will live one day at a time, this day, the day you are in now, life will be a lot easier. He did say, "I AM" (EX. 3:14). *Now* faith is.

He said to the disciples in the storm, "Why are you afraid? Take courage. I AM!" (Matt. 14:27, author's paraphrase.) Do you get it? Jesus was saying "I AM" here for you right now, and when "I AM," everything is going to be all right. Live today! Worrying about yesterday or tomorrow steals today. You have been given grace for today. Grace for tomorrow will not come until tomorrow, and yesterday's grace is all used up. Grace is an enablement, the favor and power of the Holy Spirit to help you do whatever needs to be done. But we cannot get grace ahead of time and store it up, so to speak.

Remember the Israelites in the wilderness? God supernaturally fed them on a daily basis by raining their food out of the heavens. They called it "manna." Like us, they wanted to make sure that they would have enough for tomorrow as well as today. They wanted to have tomorrow taken care of just in case God forgot to be miraculous the next morning, but God forbid them to collect more than they needed for any one given day, except on the Sabbath. And if they did collect more than needed to live one day at a time, the excess rotted.

Stop and think about this awhile. It is a powerful example that we can apply to our lives today. When you are reasoning, worrying and fretting, are you trying to store up manna for tomorrow? Your Father in heaven wants you to trust Him for tomorrow. Proverbs 3:5 (AMP) says to trust in the Lord with all your heart and mind (thoughts) and to not rely on your own understanding.

I once read the following illustration. Two men were in prison for their testimony about Jesus Christ. They were to be burned at the stake the next morning. One of them was an elderly saint who had much experience in the ways of God. The other was a young man who loved the Lord very much but did not have a lot of experience in God's ways.

The young man struck a match to light a candle as evening settled in, and the room was getting dark. In the process, he burned his finger. He began to get very upset and to scream in fear saying, "If burning my finger hurts this badly, I will never be able to stand being burned at the stake." The elderly saint comforted him with these words, "Son, God did not ask you to burn your finger, so He did not give you grace. He is asking you to make this sacrifice of your life, and you can be assured that when morning comes, the grace will be there to do what you need to do."

You see, the elder, more experienced saint knew from years of walking with the Lord that without fail when morning came, the grace of God would be there. Therefore, he was comforted in the *now*, because he had faith in the *now*, that tomorrow the ability (*grace*) would be there.

You can see from this example that faith delivers us from "reasonings." Faith does not have to figure out the future. Faith rests because it knows that God will deliver tomorrow's manna tomorrow. I really encourage you not to waste today trying to figure out *(reasoning)* what happened in the past or what is going to happen in the future.

As I once read: Yesterday is like a canceled check, tomorrow is like a promissory note and today is the only ready cash you have. *Use it wisely!*

5

❧

IF ONLY

*T*he Apostle Paul teaches in Philippians that we are to let go of what lies in the past and press on to what lies ahead. (PHIL. 3:13.) How do we hang on to the past if not in our thoughts? I believe we can spin our wheels living in the past mentally, and we should be spending that energy on today.

Do you ever relive past mistakes over and over? Do you ever think, "Why did I do that? Oh, *if only* I would not have said it or done it." Or, "*If only* I would have done such and such." Be careful of the "*if onlys.*"

Perhaps you thought you were doing everything the way it needed to be done and still things turned out sour. You might wonder, "Why did things turn out the way they did? Why, God, why? I just do not understand. I have to figure this out! I just cannot stand not to know! Oh, I am so confused!"

Does your thinking sound like this? May I be very blunt? *You are tormenting yourself!* I spent years doing this. *It does not work!* There were and are many things in my past that I did not and still do not understand. But I thank God that He finally got the message to me that I needed to let go of what was behind and press on to what was ahead. Now I enjoy a tremendous amount of peace.

The Word says in Isaiah 26:3, God will "keep him in perfect peace, whose mind is stayed on" Him. It does not say he whose mind is busy reasoning and trying to figure everything out will be kept in perfect peace.

There are many apparently unjust, unfair things that happen. In my past, as there were probably in yours, lots of things happened to me that were unfair—things that caused me a lot of problems, wounds and hurts that took years to get over.

I spent years in self-pity with a chip on my shoulder—bitter and resentful trying to reason out why it had happened to me. Why didn't God help me? Why didn't somebody help me?

I finally realized I was making myself miserable. I was wasting all my todays trying to understand my yesterdays. God said to me one day, "Joyce, you can be pitiful or powerful. Which do you want?"[1]

Sometimes you may even live in yesterday's victories. You can get caught up in trying to reason out what you did that made the success, so that you can do it again. I used to mentally *wallow* in my past victories. Even that can keep you from going forward. The past is the past. Whether the past had victory or defeat, it is still the past. It is gone. *Live today!*

There is nothing wrong with pleasant memories, but it is a mistake, and a big one, to *dwell* even in past victories. After each event in your life, let the curtain drop at your heels as you leave that thing and go on to the next thing God has for you. Philippians 3:13 (AMP) says, ". . . forgetting what lies behind and straining forward to what lies ahead."

---

1. Joyce has a cassette teaching tape available entitled "Turn Self-Pity Into Power."

I want to repeat again for you to be cautious of the *"if onlys."* If a bad thing happened, we can think *"if only"* I would not have done it that way. If a good thing happened, we can be found thinking *"if only"* I could make it happen again.

Forget the past! Do not try to reason it out anymore. Make a decision *now* to go forward.

6

ॐ

WHAT IF?

*A*nother mental arrow (the Bible in Eph. 6:16 calls them "fiery darts") that Satan throws against you is the fear-producing statement, *what if!*

What if the money does not come? *What if* you get hurt? *What if* you get seriously ill? *What if* you lose your job? *What if* you are lonely all your life? Or, how about this one, *what if* you are not hearing from God? *What if* you make a mistake? *What if* you fail? *What if* they laugh at you? *What if* you get rejected? And on and on the list goes. Do you recognize the thinking pattern?

The *what ifs* are another form of trying to figure everything out by "reasonings." *What if* comes and is usually followed by a train of thoughts that present a very grim picture. *What if* takes us into the future and causes us to dread things that have not even happened and probably never will unless we create them through fear.

What if causes confusion just like *if only.* They are both forms of thinking that we are not to indulge in. They are both certainly included in 2 Corinthians 10 under "theories and reasonings" (AMP) and "imaginations" (KJV), all of which are to be cast down.

Let me give you a practical example of what I mean. At one point, our ministry was in need of a building in which to hold our weekly meeting. The building we used to meet in for more than five years was being torn down in approximately two years, and a shopping center was to be put in its place. We were seeking a facility that would house our offices and our weekly meeting with ample space to have nurseries, the children's ministry and room to grow in, etc. We also needed to have about 300 parking spaces.

Now, one would think that should not be too hard to find; however, it was not as easy as you might think. We had been looking for two years. We had exhausted every possibility known to us. It really looked as if we had come to a dead end.

The devil threw fiery darts such as: "*What if* the two years go by, and you still do not have a place?" Or a fiery dart came that carried the message: "*If only* you would have taken such and such property when it was available so cheap, you wouldn't be in this situation. *What if* you missed God? *If only* you knew more about this kind of thing, then you would probably know what to do. *What if* you buy property and then cannot get the permits you need? *What if* you pay too much then find something better and at a better price?"

I often thank God that I had been delivered from the bondage of reasoning before the issue of needing a building came up for us. If the same situation would have occurred a few years sooner, I would have really made myself miserable, confused and fearful by trying to figure out all these things.

Now, I am able to believe that our steps are ordered of the Lord. (PS. 37:23.) We are praying and trusting God, and we want His will. Therefore, He will lead us to the right place at the right time. God is usually not early, but He is *never* late. There were various deals that we had tried and tried to work out in the past that just would not work out, no matter how hard we tried. However, at the right time, God did provide us with a great place to rent, and He will continue to provide each step of the way.

Now I can look at the different situations and see why they would not have been right. But at the time, it seemed as if I was trying so hard to find a place and nothing was working. Nothing will work when we are out of God's timing trying to *make* something happen.

God really does know what He is doing. He really is in control. I can relax and know that even if I do not know what I am going to do, I do know the One Who does know.

How about you? Do you know Jesus? Then you also know the Omniscient, Omnipotent, Omnipresent God— the One Who is all powerful, all knowing, and everywhere all the time.

Relax! *What if* you reason and reason, finally think you have it all figured out, and God surprises you and does it a totally different way? Then all that time would have been wasted. Haven't you wasted enough time in reasoning and confusion?

Here is an idea: *What if* you just relax and let God be God?

7

❧

DON'T BE LED
BY YOUR HEAD

I was praying for discernment to function in my life in a much greater measure. Actually, I had been praying about it for quite some time when the Holy Spirit said to me, "You will never operate in discernment, Joyce, until you lay reasoning aside."

First Corinthians 2:14–16 tells us plainly that the natural man does not understand the spiritual man. The Lord used this Scripture to get His point across. If my spirit brought forth discernment and my head reasoned as to whether it made sense or not, I would never make any progress. Why? Because of what 1 Corinthians 2:14 says: The natural man does not understand the things of the spirit because they are spiritually discerned. Your spirit knows things that your head does not know.

If you are a born-again child of God, then the Holy Spirit dwells in your human spirit. I believe the Holy Spirit attempts to convey many things to us that we reject because we operate so much in the soulish realm.

I will give you an example. One morning as I was getting dressed to go to one of our weekly "Life In The Word" meetings, I started thinking about the woman who ran our ministry of helps at that particular meeting and about how faithful she had been. A desire rose up in my heart to do something for her to bless her in some way.

I said, "Lord, what can I do for Ruth Ann?" I felt a strong impression, or you might say, *I just knew* I was to give her a new red dress that was hanging in my closet. I had purchased the dress three months earlier. Although I really liked it, every time I thought about wearing it, I just had no desire to put it on. It was still hanging in the plastic bag from the store with all the tags on it. Ruth Ann was a little larger framed woman than I am, but interestingly enough, I had bought the dress one size bigger than I normally wear because they did not have one in my size.

Because of the way the dress was styled, I did not think anyone would notice that it was a little big on me.

Well, when this strong desire rose up in my spirit to give her the dress, my head said, "But Lord, that dress is new." Notice that as my head, my natural man, argues with my spirit, the argument really makes no sense at all. Then I said, "Surely you are not telling me to give away a dress that is brand new." Actually, if I had thought about God's character, His generosity and His excellence, I would have known God is more likely to tell me to give away a dress that is new than one that is worn out.

King David said in 2 Samuel 24:24 (AMP) regarding the building of the temple, "I will not offer burnt offerings to the Lord my God of that which costs me nothing." You see, our flesh does not mind parting with something that means "nothing" to us. However, a new red dress is a different story. In order to give that away, I had to sacrifice.

My last argument was really funny. I said, "Lord, I bought these pretty red and silver earrings to go with that dress." I said it in a rather sulky, self-pity tone. I suppose I was hoping the Lord would feel sorry for me. His answer was complete silence to my first two arguments and to my third comment about the earrings. He let me know I could also give her the earrings if keeping them without the dress was a problem.

God does not argue with us. He tells us *by a desire, a knowing, an impression on our spirit, a still, small voice, occasionally an audible voice or frequently a Scripture that is illuminated to us.* Remember, God will not lead you to do something outside His will, which is His Word. Also, be careful about being led by voices. There are many voices. Make sure your spirit bears you witness in the Holy Ghost.

My spirit bore witness to Ruth Ann having the dress, but my flesh did not want to give it up. So I kept giving God *reasons* why it did not make sense. But God did not argue with me. He had said what He had to say. If you remember what was going on in the beginning, I was thinking about Ruth Ann and what a blessing she was, and *I asked God* what I could do for her. He told me, but my head *(reasoning)* did not like it even though my spirit knew it was right. Now it was up to me to *decide.*

Well, I put the decision off. This is usually our favorite way to get out of doing what God is telling us to do without being blatantly disobedient, or *so we think.* Actually procrastination is disobedience. Good intentions are not obedience. Action taken based on God's Word is obedience.

A few weeks went by, and I forgot all about the whole incident, *but God did not.* I was praying for Ruth Ann, and I actually said the same thing to Him all over again. "God, how can I bless Ruth Ann?" There it was again. The same red dress loomed up inside me. I finally realized I was not obeying and gave her the red dress.

Actually I realized after I decided to go ahead and give it to her that I had purchased it for her to begin with, and that was why it had hung in my closet for three months, new, without me ever taking it out of the bag. The Lord, of course, knows all these things ahead of time, but we can really make a project out of obedience. This whole mess is created by the natural man not understanding the spiritual man that 1 Corinthians 2 talks about.

"Why, God, Why?" the natural man says. "Why would you want me to sacrifice? Why can't it be easy? Why does it have to be so hard?" Romans 8:6 (AMP) says that the mind of the flesh is sense and reason without the Holy Spirit. It also conveys the thought that this type of behavior steals our peace.

Just in case you have lost sight of our main goal in this book, let me remind you that I am attempting to establish that reasoning "Why, God, Why?" is one of the things that causes confusion, steals our peace and, ultimately, our joy.

Do you want to enjoy your life? Then "reasonings" will have to go!

8

⚭

"REASONINGS"
CAUSE DECEPTION

*T*he only hope of not being deceived these days is to learn to walk by the Spirit—to be led by the Spirit, not by the flesh. Satan is looking for carnal Christians who are led by their head, their emotions and their own will rather than by the Word and the Spirit. We cannot take action because we feel like it or do not feel like it. We must, for the sake of the Kingdom and for our own protection, take action that is Spirit led.

The mind likes to slot everything. It wants to find some place to put everything so that it seems to make sense and to be taken care of. We do not like unanswered questions. One of the tools the Spirit uses to crucify our flesh is unanswered questions. When we do not *know* the answer, we have to either trust God, or worry and try to figure it out.

The Holy Spirit has the job of bringing the believer to a place of maturity after Jesus saves him. A believer who can trust the Father when things do not seem to make sense is a mature believer. Therefore, God does not always give us answers to all of our questions because He is training us in trust. However, you must remember, your mind is very opposed to this whole plan of God. Your mind is natural and is considered to be part of the *flesh* until it is renewed and learns to *think spiritually*.

Romans 8 speaks of the mind of the flesh and the mind of the Spirit. Galatians 5:17 (AMP) says that the flesh is opposed to the Spirit, and the Spirit is opposed to the flesh and that they continually withstand and are in conflict with one another.

Let's go back to our original thought at the beginning of this chapter. The natural mind wants to *put* everything somewhere and slot it in a nice little bin where it fits and does not leave us not knowing.

We had a long row of mailbox slots at our office at one time. Each one had an employee name on it. When I wanted to send an instruction or message to a certain employee, I put a note in that employee's mailbox slot. Once in a while, something I had asked an employee to do did not get done, and upon checking, I would discover that I had placed the note in a wrong slot. Sometimes I had even placed it in an empty slot that had no one's name on it.

The Lord used those mailbox slots to teach me this lesson I am trying to teach you. He showed me that just like I put things in the wrong slot at the office, I also sometimes put things in the wrong slot in my head. I always wanted to *put* everything somewhere in my thinking so that I had a neat little package with no loose ends floating around that I was having to trust God with. I had a *big* problem with "reasonings." I often asked, "Why, God, Why?" Therefore, I had a lot of confusion and worry and a lack of peace and joy.

I also deceived myself sometimes, the Lord showed me, because at times I thought I had a certain issue all figured out, and I would be taking action or not taking action according to what I thought. I would find out later, after I had made a mess, even though I thought I knew or understood or had it all figured out, that I really had it in a wrong slot after all.

God used Proverbs 3:7 (AMP) to bring this truth home to me: "Be not wise in your own eyes." The Lord let me know I was not half as smart as I thought I was. I am not talking about mental intelligence. I am speaking of our opinion of ourselves—we have things all figured out.

Proverbs 3:5, 6 (AMP) says:

> "Lean on, trust in, and be confident in the Lord
> with all your heart and mind and do not rely on
> your own insight or understanding. In all your
> ways know, recognize, and acknowledge Him,
> and He will direct and make straight and plain
> your paths."

When God makes it plain, you have no confusion or doubt, but if you try to reason and figure it out, you may go in circles and never really know truth. Verse 7 (AMP) says, "Be not wise in your own eyes."

Here are two ways to approach a situation: one is correct, and the other is not; one is spiritual, and the other is of the flesh. Let's say someone gives me a personal prophecy that I do not really understand, or say I have a spiritual dream I do not understand. I can go to the Father and say, "Father, I do not understand this. I would like to understand, so I am asking You to give me revelation. Give me understanding."

Then I place the thing that I do not understand on a shelf. In other words, I do not think about it anymore. I put it in God's hands. If and when He is ready to give me understanding, He will take it off my shelf and bring it back to my remembrance. John 14:26 says the Holy Spirit brings things to our remembrance. He will cause me by revelation to *know* what I never could have figured out.

The second way I could handle the same situation, if I had a dream or a prophecy I did not understand, would be to start really trying to figure it out. I could talk to a lot of people about it and get their opinion. I might add that most of them would probably have a different opinion, so that would add to my confusion. Then, when I got something all figured out, I would begin to take action. But really, if I would be still and honest with myself, I would have to say I did not have peace inside. If I kept trying to make something happen based on what "I thought" about this dream, prophecy or vision, *I would end up making a very large mess.*

Remember, "reasonings" cause confusion. I am not

saying that we should not think about issues, but there is a difference in meditating on something long enough to see if you get understanding and trying so hard to figure it out that you get genuinely confused.

When you feel confused, let that be a warning signal to you that you are handling something the wrong way.

9

❦

CONFUSION STEALS YOUR JOY

In this final chapter, let me reestablish that *confusion is not from God*. First Corinthians 14:33 says, "God is not the author of confusion." Colossians 3:15 (AMP) says to let peace be the "umpire" that makes the decisions in our lives. Peace, as the umpire, says what is in and what is out.

Confusion is the exact opposite of peace. "Confusion" means all mixed together, unclean, jumbled up, to mistake one thing for another or to blur. "Peace" means order, undisturbed, inner contentment, serene. If a person does not have peace, he or she will not have joy. Jesus said in John 10:10 (AMP) that the thief comes to steal, kill and destroy, but He, Jesus, came that we might "have and enjoy life."

I decided a few years ago that I was going to enjoy God

and enjoy life. If Jesus died for me so I could not only have life but also enjoy it, then I should attempt to enjoy it.

In John 15 it is reported how Jesus taught on the life of abiding, which refers to entering into the rest of God. In verses 1–10, He speaks of the life of abiding. Then in verse 11 (AMP), He says,

> "I have told you these things, that My joy and delight may be in you, and that your joy and gladness may be of full measure and complete and overflowing."

It sure sounds like He wants us to enjoy life. Confusion will certainly prevent that goal from coming to pass.

In closing, I want to encourage you to make a decision to live in joy, not confusion and turmoil. You will need to give up *"reasonings."* Each time we gain a spiritual victory we are required to give up something of the fleshly nature. The nature of the flesh is "to try to figure things out." The nature of the Spirit is "to trust God to reveal the answer in His timing."

If you will give up "reasonings," I truly believe you will reap *peace* and *joy.*

EXPERIENCING A NEW LIFE

❦

*I*f you have never invited Jesus to be your Lord and Savior, I invite you to do so now. You can pray this prayer, and if you are really sincere about it, you will experience a new life in Christ.

Father God, I believe Jesus Christ is your Son, the Savior of the world. I believe He died on the cross for me, and He bore all of my sins. He went to hell in my place and triumphed over death and the grave. I believe Jesus was resurrected from the dead and is now seated at your right hand. I need You, Jesus. Forgive my sins, save me, come to live inside me. I want to be born again.

Now believe Jesus is living in your heart. You are forgiven and made righteous, and when Jesus comes, you will go to heaven.

Find a good church that is teaching God's Word and begin to grow in Christ. Nothing will change in your life without knowledge of God's Word.

Beloved,

John 8:31, 32 (AMP) says, "If you abide in My word . . . you are truly My disciples. And you will know the Truth, and the Truth will set you free."

I exhort you to take hold of God's Word, plant it deep in your heart, and according to 2 Corinthians 3:18, as you look into the Word, you will be transformed into the image of Jesus Christ.

Write and let me know you have accepted Jesus, and ask for a free booklet on how to begin your new life in Christ.

With Love,

Joyce

About the Author

∞

Joyce Meyer has been teaching the Word of God since 1976 and in full-time ministry since 1980. She is the best-selling author of more than fifty inspirational books, including *How to Hear from God*, *Knowing God Intimately*, and *Battlefield of the Mind*. She has also released thousands of teaching cassettes and a complete video library. Joyce's *Enjoying Everyday Life* radio and television programs are broadcast around the world, and she travels extensively conducting conferences. Joyce and her husband, Dave, are the parents of four grown children and make their home in St. Louis, Missouri.

To contact the author write:

Joyce Meyer Ministries
P. O. Box 655
Fenton, Missouri 63026
or call: (636) 349-0303
Internet Address: www.joycemeyer.org

*Please include your testimony or help received from this book
when you write. Your prayer requests are welcome.*

To contact the author
in Canada, please write:
Joyce Meyer Ministries Canada, Inc.
Lambeth Box 1300
London, ON N6P 1T5
or call: (636) 349-0303

In Australia, please write:
Joyce Meyer Ministries-Australia
Locked Bag 77
Mansfield Delivery Centre
Queensland 4122
or call: 07 3349 1200

In England, please write:
Joyce Meyer Ministries
P. O. Box 1549
Windsor
SL4 1GT
Or call: (0) 1753-831102

Joyce Meyer Titles

Starting Your Day Right
Beauty for Ashes Revised Edition
How to Hear from God
Knowing God Intimately
The Power of Forgiveness
The Power of Determination
The Power of Being Positive
The Secrets of Spiritual Power
The Battle Belongs to the Lord
Secrets to Exceptional Living
Eight Ways to Keep the Devil Under Your Feet
Teenagers are People Too
Filled with the Spirit
Celebration of Simplicity
The Joy of Believing Prayer
Never Lose Heart
Being the Person God Made You to Be
A Leader in the Making
"Good Morning, This is God!" Gift Book
Jesus—Name Above All Names
"Good Morning, This is God!" Daily Calendar
Help Me—I'm Married!
Reduce Me to Love
Be Healed in Jesus' Name
How to Succeed at Being Yourself
Eat and Stay Thin
Weary Warriors, Fainting Saints
Life in the Word Journal
Life in the Word Devotional

Be Anxious for Nothing
Be Anxious for Nothing Study Guide
Straight Talk on Loneliness
Straight Talk on Fear
Straight Talk on Insecurity
Straight Talk on Discouragement
Straight Talk on Worry
Straight Talk on Depression
Straight Talk on Stress
Don't Dread
Managing Your Emotions
Healing the Brokenhearted
Me and My Big Mouth
Me and My Big Mouth! Study Guide
Prepare to Prosper
Do It Afraid!
Expect a Move of God in Your Life . . . Suddenly!
Enjoying Where You Are on the Way to Where You Are Going
The Most Important Decision You Will Ever Make
When, God When?
Why, God Why?
The Word, the Name, the Blood
Battlefield of the Mind
Battlefield of the Mind Study Guide
Tell Them I Love Them
Peace
The Root of Rejection
Beauty for Ashes
If Not for the Grace of God
If Not for the Grace of God Study Guide

CPSIA information can be obtained at www.ICGtesting.com
Printed in the USA
BVOW08s2014060214

344145BV00001B/27/P